Winnie the Pooh

NATURE'S TRUE COLORS

By K. Emily Hutta

Illustrated by
Carson Van Osten, John Kurtz
& the Disney Storybook Artists

It was a brisk, bright, blustery day in the Hundred-Acre Wood. Piglet was pushed this way and that by the wind as he made his way to the home of his good friend Winnie the Pooh.

Piglet was just about to knock when Pooh's door burst open.

"I was . . . would you . . ." a startled Piglet began, trying to gather his thoughts. "What I meant to say is . . . hello, Pooh! Don't you think today is just the right sort of day for a ramble?"

"A . . . yes . . . oh, indeed . . . hello, Piglet!" said Pooh. "I was just about to go somewhere, but I would much prefer a ramble. Because when you're going nowhere in particular, well, you are quite sure to get there."

The sky on this day was so blue, the color so splendidly clear and true, that Piglet and Pooh hadn't gone very far before they just had to stop and admire it.

"Isn't the sky glorious?" Piglet exclaimed, tilting his head so far back that Pooh had to catch him before he tipped over completely.

"Have you ever happened to notice," asked Pooh, setting Piglet upright, "how many different colors the sky can be?"

"Oh, yes!" Piglet said. "Sometimes the sky is so dark it looks purple!"

"Then there's that gentle sort of grayish color when it rains," said Pooh.

The path the friends were following wound through a little meadow, where golden grasses made a soft swishing sound as the wind blew through them.

Pooh and Piglet stopped to listen.

"Piglet," whispered Pooh, "I would like to say that you are a splendid rambling partner. You know just when to go and when to stop. I think a good ramble requires plenty of stopping, don't you?"

"Oh, I agree, Pooh," whispered Piglet. "If you go too much or go too soon, well, you might miss something."

"Like these gold-colored waves in the grass," said Pooh, "with their quiet little shushing sound."

Shhhhhhhhhhhhhh, said the wind in the grass. *Shhhhhhhhhhh*.

"I would have been very sorry to miss that, Piglet," whispered Pooh.

After some time, the path climbed a small hill—so Piglet and Pooh climbed it, too.

The wind carried the sharp, sweet scent of ripe apples, which filled their noses—and then their minds—as they climbed.

"I was just thinking, Piglet," said Pooh, whose mind and tummy very often had the same thoughts, "that this would be a very good time for a smackerel."

At the top of the hill, Piglet and Pooh saw an apple tree, its branches heavy with shiny red fruit. They agreed that this was a splendid stopping place.

"I think—*crunch*—that red apples are my favorite," Pooh said.

"Isn't that—*nibble, nibble*—what you said about Rabbit's little green apples yesterday?" asked Piglet.

"Yes," said Pooh.

Eventually, the path ran down the other side of the hill—so Piglet and Pooh ran, too. But Pooh tripped and started rolling—and although he didn't mean to bowl Piglet over, he did anyway.

This might have seemed like an unfortunate circumstance if Piglet hadn't noticed a frog. It was tiny and mud brown, and it would have been quite invisible if someone—even a rather short someone—had been standing up.

So Piglet and Pooh stayed where they were and took a long look around. At the little bog with its sleek, still, brown water. At the silver-winged dragonflies shimmering across the surface. At the dark green moss carpeting the banks.

"If you didn't look closely, you might think this was a dull and drab-ish sort of place," said Pooh.

"Yes," agreed Piglet, "but only if you didn't look closely."

In good time, Piglet and Pooh felt ready to go again. They soon came to a stream lined with trees in glorious autumn colors.

"Do you see that orange one over there, Pooh?" Piglet asked, pointing to a fiery orange leaf. "I think it's absolutely splendid."

"It seems that just last week the leaves were all green," Pooh said.

"I have always liked seeing the leaves change color in the autumn," said Pooh. "What I never noticed before is that the stream changes color, too."

Piglet looked where Pooh was pointing, and, indeed, the water was full of swirls of color. Lavender. Turquoise. Pink. There were rocks in the stream with red and yellow stripes, plants with blue and white dots, and logs with purple streaks!

"What are you two looking at?" asked Eeyore.

"Oh, hello, Eeyore!" said Pooh. "Did you know that the stream changes colors in the autumn—just like the leaves?"

It's not at all surprising that Eeyore wanted to see for himself—but one thing led to another, as things often do, and the next thing Eeyore knew, his bow was in the stream. When it came back out, it was orange, red, and lime green!

Then Pooh dipped his toe into the water, and it came out lavender and fuchsia and blue!

"Now we're changing colors, too!" said Pooh. "This is a very peculiar sort of autumn."

Eeyore, Piglet, and Pooh were discussing what to do when they came across Rabbit and Roo peering into Rabbit's watering can.

"Is something wrong, Rabbit?" Piglet asked.

"It's my watering can," Rabbit said. "The water has painted it colors."

"Just like my bow," Eeyore said glumly.

"Not to mention my toe," said Pooh.

"I want to change colors, too!" said Roo.

"I'm sure Kanga likes you just the way you are," Eeyore said, holding Roo by the tail to keep him from jumping into the stream.

"There's something very strange going on around here," Rabbit said. "And I'm going to find out what it is."

"Me, too!" said Piglet, Pooh, Eeyore, and Roo.

Just then Owl called out from a nearby tree. "Hello there! Did any of you happen to notice . . . ?"

"Yes!" Rabbit said.

"And do you happen to know . . . ?"

"No!" said Rabbit. "But we're going to get to the bottom of it."

"The Bottom?" Piglet squeaked anxiously. "I'm not at all sure I want to get to the Bottom."

"This way," Rabbit said, marching off along the bank of the stream. Eeyore followed. Roo leaped ahead and bounded back to report on more multi-colored water and strangely painted mud patches. Piglet reluctantly brought up the rear with Pooh and Owl.

"You'll let me know if we're getting near the Bottom, won't you Pooh?" Piglet asked nervously.

"Of course, Piglet," said Pooh. "I just hope I'll know it when I see it."

Piglet and Pooh were on the lookout for the Bottom—which might have been behind or under or near—when they rounded a bend and bumped into Eeyore.

"Why are we stopping?" Piglet asked anxiously. "Have we found the Bottom?"

"I don't know," Eeyore said. "But we have found Tigger."

Tigger was fast asleep in a shady spot on the bank of the stream. All around him, paintings were drying in the wind. Paintbrushes were scattered on the ground, and jars of uncovered paint were tipped over, some of them spilling into the stream.

"I think we can deduce what happened here," Owl said.

"Yes, and I think we can figure it out, too," said Pooh.

Rabbit shook Tigger awake.

"Look what you've done!" Rabbit said.

"I know," said Tigger. "They're paintings. Would you like one to hang above your fireplace, Long Ears?"

"I'm not talking about the paintings . . ." Rabbit sputtered.

"Although they are lovely, Tigger," Piglet said.

"I'm talking about this mess," Rabbit said. "Look at the stream, the rocks, the plants, the logs. Their colors are all wrong."

Tigger looked around him. "Art can be very messy."

"Yes, but your mess has become everyone else's mess," Rabbit said. "Even Mother Nature's!"

Then, he showed Tigger his watering can. Eeyore showed him his bow. And Pooh fell over showing him his toe.

"I'm very sorry to see how much mess one tigger can make," Tigger said in a very sorry-sounding way. "I'll never paint another picture."

"It's not the pictures that are the problem," Owl said.

"I think it's when you accidentally painted nature that you got into trouble," said Roo.

"Oh, yes," said Pooh. "I agree. Piglet and I were quite happy with nature's colors the way they were."

"Do you suppose you've learned your lesson?" Rabbit asked.

"Absotively, posilutely, Long Ears," Tigger said. "No more stripedy stripes and polka dotties on anything but tiggers and paintings!"

"I'll get the paintbrushes," Owl said.

"You might as well put them in here," Rabbit said, offering his watering can. "It's already got paint in it."

Everyone pitched in to clean up the stream.

There was so much cleaning to do that it was late in the day by the time Piglet and Pooh set off toward home. The evening sky was streaked with vivid shades of orange and gold—casting a soft glow on everything in the Hundred-Acre Wood.

Piglet sighed happily. "Have you ever seen anything more glorious?"

"It reminds me of the color of honey," said Pooh. "Which happens to be one of my tummy's favorite colors."

"I think nature paints all the colors we really need," Piglet said, stopping to gaze up at the blazing sky. "Don't you think so, Pooh?"

"Yes," said Pooh, catching Piglet as he started to tip over backward. "I truly do."

Nature

Wonders to see, smell, touch, and hear;
Nature delights us all through the year.
With beauty that's ours to enjoy and protect,
Nature deserves our love and respect.

Destination Unknown

When you're walking with a friend
And listening to the breeze,
It matters not which way you choose,
There is only you to please.

When you're neither here nor there,
Don't wonder where you're going.
On any great adventure,
The best part is not knowing!

Nature Activity

"Nature's True Colors" takes us on an autumn ramble with Piglet and Pooh. Going nowhere in particular, the two friends discover the joys of a day spent in nature. They admire the color of the sky, the sound of the wind, the smell (and taste) of ripe apples. Piglet and Pooh also see what can happen when we aren't careful to protect nature from the mistakes we sometimes make. When Tigger made a mess and didn't clean up after himself, his mess spread to nature—and his friends.

When we appreciate nature, we want to protect it. Next time you're outside, take the time to really look and listen and smell and feel. What do you see? Do you see colors you didn't notice before? Do you see shapes in the clouds or worms in the dirt? What do you hear? Do you hear bees buzzing or water gurgling? Do you hear the sound of the breeze in the trees? What do you feel? Do you feel the warmth of the sun on your face? The bite of snow on your fingers? What do you smell? Do you smell pine trees or strawberries or roses?

The more you pay attention to nature, the more amazed you'll be by what you discover. Just like Piglet and Pooh.

At Kohl's, we believe the simple act of caring creates a sense of community. Thanks to people like you, over the past 10 years Kohl's Cares for Kids ® has raised millions of dollars to support children in the communities we serve. Throughout the year, Kohl's sells special Kohl's Cares for Kids merchandise with 100% of the net profit benefiting children's health and education initiatives nationwide.

Kohl's Cares for Kids is our way of supporting our customers and improving children's lives. So when you turn the pages of this book, remember you're not only reading a fun-filled adventure, you're also helping make a difference in the life of a child.

For more information about Kohl's Cares for Kids programs, visit www.kohlscorporation.com.

PWC-SFICOC-260
FOR TEXT PAPER ONLY

For more Disney Press fun, visit www.disneybooks.com